GRAFFITI 1: The Scrawl of the Wild

GRAFFITI 2: The Walls of the World

GRAFFITI 3: The Golden Graffiti Awards

Collected and compiled by

ROGER KILROY

Wall-to-wall illustrations

by McLACHLAN

CHANCELLOR
PRESS

Graffiti: The Scrawl of the Wild first published in 1979 by Corgi Books
Graffiti 2: The Walls of the World first published in 1980 by Corgi Books
Graffiti 3: The Golden Graffiti Awards first published in 1981 by Corgi Books

This collected volume first published in 1994 by Chancellor Press
an imprint of Reed Consumer Books Limited
Michelin House, 81 Fulham Road, London SW3 6RB
and Auckland, Singapore and Toronto

ISBN 1 85152 677 3

Graffiti: The Scrawl of the Wild:	Text Material © 1979 Roger Kilroy
	Illustrations ©1979 Edward McLachlan
Graffiti 2: The Walls of the World:	Text Material © 1980 Roger Kilroy
	Illustrations © 1980 Edward McLachlan
Graffiti 3: The Golden Graffiti Awards:	Text Material ©1981 Roger Kilroy
	Illustrations © 1981 Edward McLachlan

A CIP catalogue record for this book is available from the British Library

Printed by Cox & Wyman Ltd

CONTENTS

GRAFFITI 1:

The Scrawl of the Wild

CONTENTS

Happiness is a white wall
and a magic marker

Ever since Man could write he's written on walls. There is no form
of literature so old or so universal as graffiti. It's been around
since the days of the cave-painters and looks like being with us for
the rest of time.

Graffiti can be about anything, but more often than not it's
about sex. You get philosophical graffiti, political graffiti, protest
graffiti, racist graffiti, graffiti about graffiti, (even graffiti that
manages to be both about graffiti **and** racist at the same time:
DOWN WITH GRAFFITI! **Yeah, down with all Italians!**), but
for every example of graffiti that doesn't touch on any aspect of
sex you'll find a dozen that do. It's always been the same, and if
you don't believe me take a trip to Pompeii and read some writing
on the wall that's almost a thousand years old:

Festus hic fuituit cum Sodalibus

Meaning 'this is the spot where Festus made it with Sodalibus'.
it's one of the very much more innocent samples of Pompeiian
wall gossip.
And if you can't get to Pompeii this year, when you're next in
London make your way to Chancery Lane and seek out the
window ledge on which was etched in the year 1719:

Here did I lay my Celia down;
I got the pox and she got half a crown.

And just as sex and our bodily functions seem to inspire the
bulk of the world's graffiti, so the lavatory appears to be the place
where we are most often inspired:

7

'There once was a fellow named Rafferty
Who went to a gentleman's laffertry,
    When he saw the sight
    He said, 'Newton was right,
This must be the centre of grafferty!'

Graffiti can be found in the unlikeliest of places — in the
Reading Room of the British Museum: 'It's a funny old world.
Signed, Karl Marx'; on an Egyptian pyramid: 'I've got pharoahs
at the bottom of my garden too'; at the American Embassy in
London: 'Remember, Yanks, if it wasn't for us British you'd all
have been Spanish'; inside the Vatican: 'Celibacy is not an
inherited characteristic' — but the likeliest place to find it is in a
lavatory, and in a public lavatory at that. It's not so much fun
doing it on your bathroom wall at home.

In the course of preparing this book I have visited scores of
public lavatories. I have escaped both arrest and infection, but I
haven't been able to avoid bad language. The lavatory wall, after
all, is the home of obscenity. As one graffitist put it on the door of
the staff lavatory at a school in Manchester, 'Take the four-letter
word out of the classroom and restore it to its rightful place.
Here.' If you don't like rude words, don't worry. I have confined
them to the last three chapters, to be found between pages 86 and
107, and I suggest you tear them out and send them to the vicar
right away.

The lavatory is a popular place for graffiti not only because
there we usually have time to spare, but also, and more
significantly, because in the lavatory we are usually alone. It is a
private occupation and one that can be indulged in with con-
fidence because all graffiti is essentially anonymous. There has
been one great exception to this rule and that's my namesake,
Kilroy. During the Second World War, James J. Kilroy, of
Halifax, Massachusetts, was employed at the Bethlehem Steel
Company's Quincy shipyard, inspecting tanks and other parts of
warships under construction. To satisfy his superiors that he was
performing his duties, Mr. Kilroy scribbled in yellow crayon the
words 'KILROY WAS HERE' on everything he inspected.
Soon the phrase began to appear in various unrelated places and
Mr. Kilroy believes the fourteen thousand shipyard workers who
entered the armed services were responsible for its subsequent
world-wide use.

Almost all graffiti is anonymous. Almost all of it is pretty
banal as well. I have tried to reproduce graffiti that is neither
totally inane or simply obscene. And I have tried too to avoid

pseudo-graffiti, the sort that wits work on for weeks before writing on the wall or clever media men have teams of writers thinking up so that they can be printed on buttons and badges. All the bits of graffiti that you find in the pages that follow have been sighted on real walls by real people.

We know graffiti is something millions do and we know, by and large, where they do it. But why do they do it? You'll find all sorts of answers in weightier tomes than this — especially in **Graffiti** by Robert Reisner (USA, 1974) and **Graffiti** by Richard Freeman (UK, 1968), a pair of volumes, both brilliant and profound, from which I have culled a number of my examples) — but rather than talk of graffiti as 'environmental resistance' or 'the liberation of the aggressive impulse' I prefer to answer the question by quoting one of the very first bits of graffiti I ever collected. I saw it in the lavatory at Baker Street underground station:

Why write on a wall?
Because it's there.

Up with Down!

No doubt about it, brevity is the soul of wit and many of the best bits of graffiti are the short, sharp slogans that pack a punch and promote a cause. Some have found their way onto buttons ('If I'm awake, try me. If I'm asleep, wake me'), some have been emblazoned on T-shirts ('People who lives in glass blouses shouldn't show bones'), some have been printed onto postcards ('You don't have to be mad to work here — but it helps'), but the best work best scrawled on the place where they belong: the wall.

11

12

13

If at first you
don't succeed — CHEAT!

Don't hate yourself
in the morning — sleep till noon.

VISIT YOUR
MOTHER TODAY.
MAYBE SHE
HASN'T HAD ANY
PROBLEMS LATELY

Earn cash in your
spare time —
blackmail your
friends!

EGGHEADS OF
THE WORLD UNITE!
YOU HAVE NOTHING
TO LOSE BUT YOUR YOKE!

Hire the
morally
handicapped

15

17

18

19

DON'T SHOOT—I DON'T
WAN'T TO BE PRESIDENT!

I WAS BORN
THIS WAY—
WHAT'S YOUR
EXCUSE?

BE SECURITY CONSCIOUS
—BECAUSE 80% OF PEOPLE
ARE CAUSED BY ACCIDENT!

Conserve energy
—make love more slowly

Life, liberty and the
happiness of pursuit!

**ENJOY A GOOD LAUGH
—GO TO WORK ON A FEATHER!**

You're never alone with schizophrenia.

Support your
local police force—STEAL!

ONLY DIRTY
PEOPLE need
to wash

CLEAN EARTH
SMELLS FUNNY

Children — Beat your mother
while she is young!

The Truth is the safest Lie!

In one of the men's lavatories at the University of California at Los Angeles this message was seen:

Why do you wash these walls?
Graffiti is a learning experience.

Underneath, the lavatory attendant had added:

SO IS WASHING WALLS

You can learn a lot from a wall and there is hardly any aspect of human endeavour that is not touched on by the graffitist's somewhat cynical philosophy. For some choice examples of wall-wisdom, read on.

WHY WORRY ABOUT TOMORROW
WHEN TODAY IS SO FAR OFF?

NUDISTS ARE PEOPLE
WHO WEAR ONE-BUTTON
SUITS

The difference between this firm
and a cactus plant is that the
plant has pricks on the outside!

There's more to life
than meets the mind.

IT'S NOT THE WORK THAT GETS
ME DOWN — IT'S THE COFFEE BREAKS!

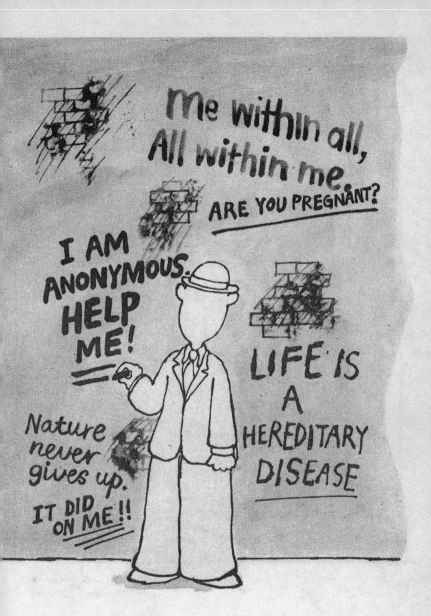

I think I exist;
therefore I exist, I think
I THINK I THINK: THEREFORE I THINK.
FOR THOSE WHO THINK LIFE IS A JOKE - JUST THINK OF THE PUNCHLINE!!
It's me and you against the world — when do we attack?
HATE!

All the world's a stage and the people on it are poorly rehearsed.

NO, JUST POORLY DIRECTED!

No, just poorly cast!

IS THERE ANY INTELLIGENT LIFE ON EARTH?

Yes, but I'm only visiting

I'd give my right arm to be ambidextrous

Those who think they know it all upset those of us who do!

PEOPLE ARE NO DAMNED GOOD

Pgychiatrists are worse

PSYCHIATRISTS AREN'T PEOPLE

What has posterity
ever done for me?

AN APPLE A DAY KEEPS
THE DOCTOR AWAY, BUT AN
ONION A DAY KEEPS EVERYONE
AWAY — ANON

THE WORLD
IS YOUR OYSTER
SO EAT IT!

Reality is a crutch!

IF YOU CAN KEEP YOUR HEAD WHEN THOSE ABOUT YOU ARE LOSING THEIRS, PERHAPS YOU'VE MISUNDERSTOOD THE SITUATION!

Alimony is paying for something you don't get!

Old soldiers never die—just young ones!

Even hypochondriacs can be ill

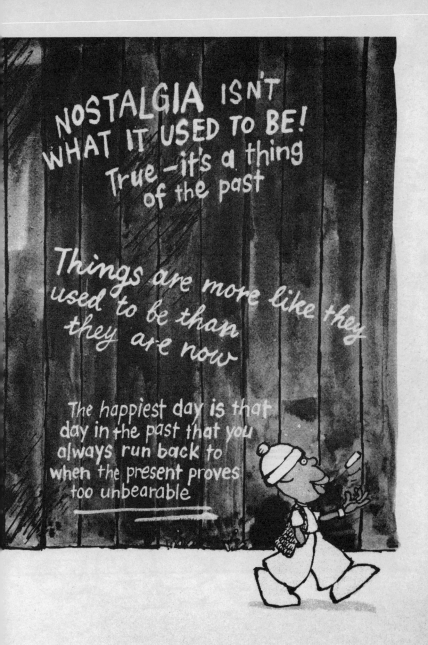

NOSTALGIA ISN'T WHAT IT USED TO BE!
True — it's a thing of the past

Things are more like they used to be than they are now

The happiest day is that day in the past that you always run back to when the present proves too unbearable

34

God is dead!!

On the whole, the graffitist steers clear of matters spiritual, but now and then he has a go at the Great Imponderables of Life and Death and Things Everlasting.

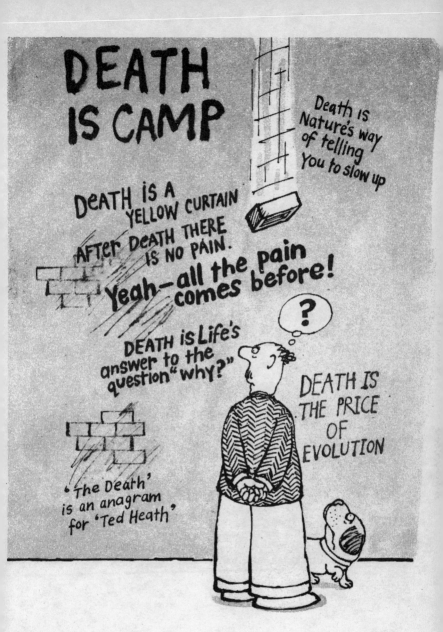

Death is the greatest kick of all
That's why they save it for last

Start an underground
movement today - Get
yourself buried alive!

The most sincere
form of criticism
is suicide - do it!

The greatest
high is
Suicide!

DEATH IS ONLY
A STATE OF MIND
Only it doesn't leave
you much time to think
about anything else!

TO KICK
THE BUCKET IS
BEYOND THE PAIL

IN CASE OF ATOMIC ATTACK...

1) Put your hands over your ears
2) Put your head between your legs.
3) Kiss your ass goodbye
    —YOU'VE HAD IT!

Venus is a star!

If it's true that the final test of fame is to have a madman believe he's you, it's at least a sign of notoriety to have your name used in a piece of graffiti. If you want to be immortal, get yourself scrawled on a wall.

Snoopy has fleas
ISAAC NEWTON COUNTS ON HIS FINGERS
William Tell wore contact lenses
PERRY MASON BRIBES JUDGES
Lassie kills chickens
QUENTIN CRISP IS STRAIGHT
Basil Brush is a poof —Bum, Bum!

Looby Loo is a lousy lay
— Andy Pandy

MARGARET THATCHER
FOR P. M.

And what about A.M. duckie?

Pinocchio is a swinger

GOLDA MEIR IS A MASOCHIST
but she speaks English!

OEDIPUS WAS THE FIRST
MAN TO PLUG THE
GENERATION GAP

Marshall McLuhan is print-orientated
Count Dracula, your Bloody Mary is ready
BATMAN LOVES ROBIN
SOCRATES EATS HEMLOCK

YOU THINK OEDIPUS HAD A PROBLEM. ADAM WAS EVE'S MOTHER!!
Hugh Hefner is a virgin
WELLINGTONS MISTRESSES WERE ALL OLD BOOTS!
This is where Napoleon tore his Bonaparte!
GRAFFITI WAS MUSSOLINI'S SECRETARY OF DEFENCE
SUPERMAN GETS INTO CLARK KENT'S PANTS EVERY MORNING

W.C. FIELDS IS ALIVE AND DRUNK IN PHILADELPHIA
LEDA LOVES SWANS
ZEUS LOVES GANYMEDE!
Little Jack Horner's problem is more serious than he thinks!
Why does Superman wear his Y-fronts over his trousers?
PIE FETISH MONTHLY

IMMANUEL KANT
BUT KUBLAI KHAN

Mickey Mouse
is gay
TRUE - DONALD DUCKIE

EUCLID WAS SQUARE

Cinderella
married
for
money

Archduke Ferdinand
found alive - First World
War a mistake!!

DONALD DUCK IS MYOPIC

HHH HHH HHH
HHH HHH III

Rasputin lives!
He's in the kitchen

MARY POPPINS
SHOULDN'T
FLY AROUND
WITHOUT PANTIES

OLENKA BOHACHEVSKY LIVES!

And quite obviously
in great seclusion

OEDIPUS — PHONE YOUR MOTHER

Julie Andrews for inner cleanliness

51

When I hear the word gun, I reach for my culture!

Since graffiti has been described as 'wall culture', it's only right that the more intellectual graffitists should turn their attentions to the worlds of art, music and literature.

RENOIR'S PAINTINGS WERE VERY MUCH TOUCH-AND-GAUGUIN

Pablo Picasso paints by numbers

BALLS BY CEZANNE

Andy Warhol stencils

BOTTICELLI WAS NO ANGEL

53

When I hear the word gun, I reach for my culture!

A WOMAN IS LIKE A PIANO
IF SHE'S NOT UPRIGHT, SHE'S GRAND.

SHAKESPEARE
EATS BACON

It can't be Donne

I've been hanging
about here for
bloody ages
—Godot

SIR THOMAS
BEECHAM DOESN'T
KNOW HIS BRASS
FROM HIS OBOE

NORMAN MAILER IS
the MASTER OF THE SINGLE ENTENDRE

That Marquis de Sade sure knew
how to hurt a guy.

CONCENTRATE ON ROUSSEAU
INSTEAD OF YOUR TROUSSEAU – Sorry I Kant

OGDEN NASH
IS TRASH

Edith Sitwell is a transvestite.
SHE'S DEAD. YOU DOPE!
O.K. Edith Sitwell is a dead transvestite.

The Whole World is going to pot!

Graffiti doesn't just deal with culture: it reflects subculture too, so there were moments in the 1960s when graffiti was crazed out of its mind.

59

OLD HIPPIES NEVER DIE
—THEY JUST TRIP AWAY

BLOW YOUR MIND
—SMOKE GUNPOWDER

GOD IS ALIVE
AND LIVING IN
A SUGAR CUBE

Come alive—you're in
the banana generation!

Reality is for people
who can't cope with drugs

BE PLACID WITH ACID

One good turn-on deserves another

Melts in your mind not in your hand!

Acid indigestion can be FUN

GRASS IS NATURE'S WAY OF SAYING "HIGH!"

ACID TAKES THE WORRY OUT OF BEING

What's a nice joint like you doing in a girl like this?

TURN ON!
TUNE IN!
DROP DEAD!

It pays to advertise
—OH YEAH?

In New York City it is now an offence to sell aerosols of paint to anyone under the age of eighteen. Obviously the authorities felt that adult graffitists weren't being given a fair chance. To graffitists, young and old, printed signs and posters in public places offer some of the greatest challenges and the most satisfying rewards.

64

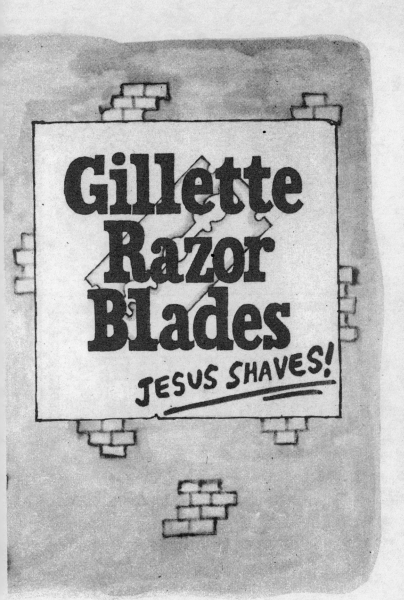

HAVE YOU TRIED PRAYER?

It's the only thing that keeps body and soul apart!

FRESH EGGS All individually laid

BURTON SHAKESPEARE COMPANY
PRESENTS

ANTHONY
AND
CLEOPATRA

THE BIGGEST
ASP DISASTER IN
THE WORLD!

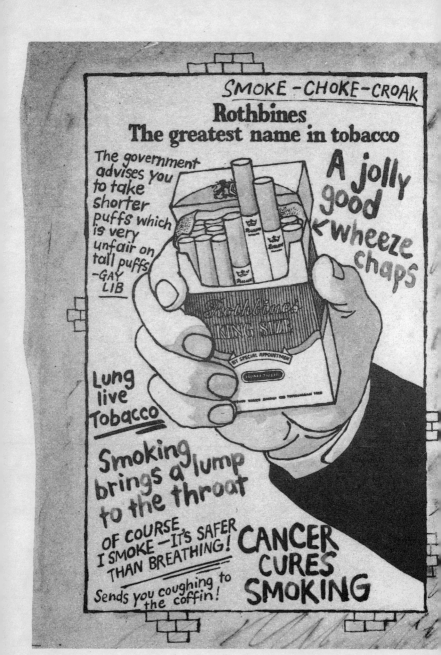

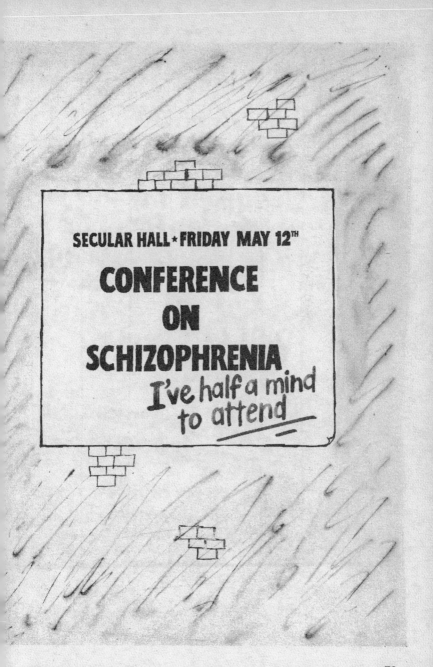

REACH A MEDIA MAN — ADVERTISE ON SWIZZLE STICKS!

I dreamed I could wear a Maidenform bra.

Twiggy

Pall Mall can't Spall!

DO RETIRING VOLKSWAGENS GO TO THE OLD VOLKS HOME?

I find Time easy to digest — except for the staples

Graffiti
rules — OK?

It began as a simple soccer fan's battle-cry,
ARSENAL RULES OK? It evolved into a national
cult, as much a craze as the yoyo, the hula-hoop and
the skateboard.

Einstein
rules relatively OK

QUEEN ELIZABETH RULES UK

DYSLEXIA RULES KO

THE LAW OF THE EXCLUDED
MIDDLE EITHER RULES OR
DOES NOT RULE OK

Amnesia
rules....er....um

Rooner Spules OK

SCHIZOPHRENIA DIVIDES
AND RULES — O.K.?

Queensbury rules — KO?

GERSHWIN RULES
— OH KAY!

Archimedes rules — Eurekay!

Mallet rules
croquet?

Pooves rule — Ooh Gay?

PESSIMISTS RULE — NOT OK!

OK
SAUCE
RULES
— HP?

TYPE RULES — OoKo

Shaking it all about rules — Hokay Cokay

Town criers
rule Okez, Okez, Okez

Lethargy rulezzzzzzzzz

FRENCH DIPLOMACY RULES — AU QUAI?

Sausage roles—OK?

SLIDE RULES $\frac{OK}{\pi}$

Absolute zero rules $0°K°$

ROGET'S THESAURUS RULES
—OK, ALL RIGHT, VERY WELL,
YOU BET, CERTAINLY

Rules rule—OK?

BrEAK RULES—OK?

ENOUGH IS ENOUGH —OK?

Adam loves Eve !

It is, of course, love that makes the world go round
and the love-struck graffitist is nothing if not
romantic.

Why does free love cost so much?

IF IT MOVES,
FONDLE IT.
Sex causes blindness
EYEBALLS!!

EVEN DIRTY OLD MEN
NEED LOVE!

PUT A LITTLE
LOVE INTO YOUR SEX LIFE

I Love Steve
— MARY

TOUGH LUCK MARY
— Steve

MAKE HASTE! MAKE LOVE!
Haste is passé and
for amateurs

CAN I HAVE
A DATE?
How about 1066?

LOVE IS A
MANY GENDERED THING.

GIRLS, WHAT DO YOU DO
WHEN YOU FIND YOUR CAT
WITH ANOTHER CAT?
Let the cats be happy
together and find a MAN!

KING KONG
TAUGHT ME
TO LOVE

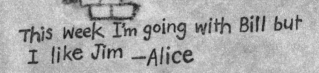

This week I'm going with Bill but
I like Jim —Alice

This week I'm going with Jim but
I like Bill —Alice

**THIS WEEK WE ARE NOT GOING
WITH ALICE — BILL AND JIM**

Help me!
I'm a Sex Junkie

If you can't cope with dirty words, stop here.

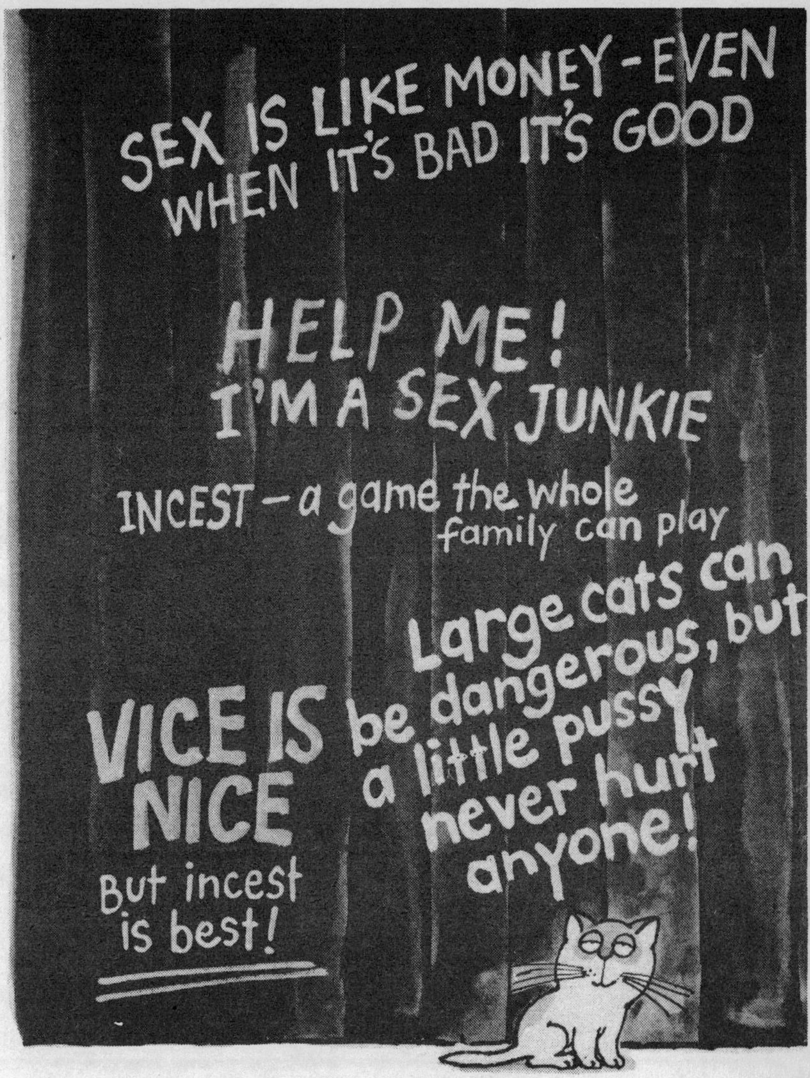
SEX IS LIKE MONEY - EVEN WHEN IT'S BAD IT'S GOOD
HELP ME! I'M A SEX JUNKIE
INCEST - a game the whole family can play
Large cats can be dangerous, but a little pussy never hurt anyone!
VICE IS NICE
But incest is best!

BE CREATIVE —INVENT A PERVERSION

BOYS MARRY VIRGINS,
MEN MARRY WOMEN.

COPULATE FOR COEXISTENCE!

Call it incest - but I want my mummy

To go together is blessed,
To come together is divine

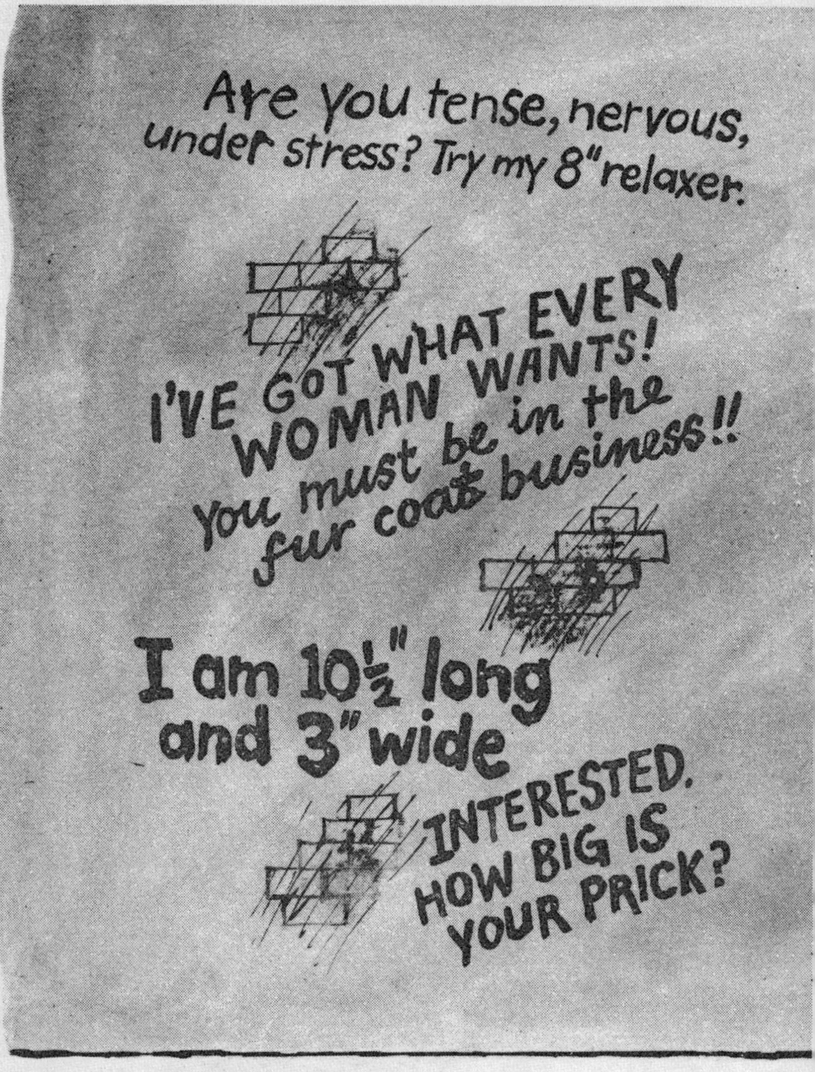
Are you tense, nervous,
under stress? Try my 8" relaxer.
I'VE GOT WHAT EVERY
WOMAN WANTS!
you must be in the
fur coat business!!
I am 10½" long
and 3" wide
INTERESTED.
HOW BIG IS
YOUR PRICK?

ONE THING ABOUT MASTURBATION. YOU DON'T HAVE TO LOOK YOUR BEST.

The difference between a stick-up and a hold-up is age.

Does the lateral coital position mean having a bit on the side?

God save the Queens!

As a variation on the traditional theme of Boy meets Girl, the gay graffitists offer us wall-thoughts on Boy meets Boy and Girl meets Girl.

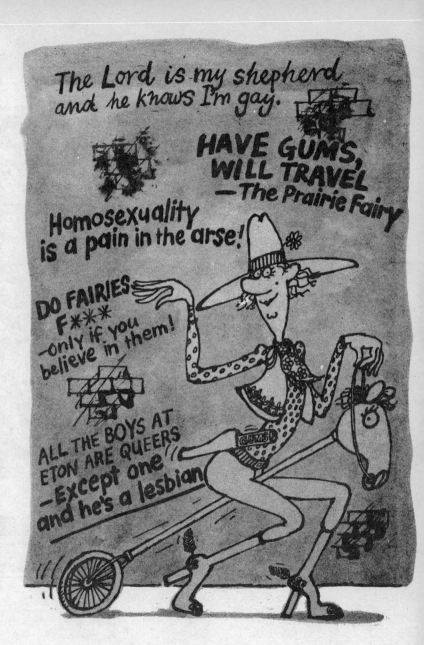

DAISIES OF THE
WORLD UNITE
—YOU HAVE NOTHING
TO LOSE BUT YOUR CHAINS

Young man, well hung with
beautiful body is willing
to do anything.
P.S. If you see this, Bill, don't
bother to call, its only me, Tony

Lenny is a
stupid faget!

I MAY BE STUPID BUT
AT LEAST I CAN SPELL FAGGET.

Dr. Strangelove or how
I learned to love the bum ———→

Veni, Vidi, Wiwi.

At last.

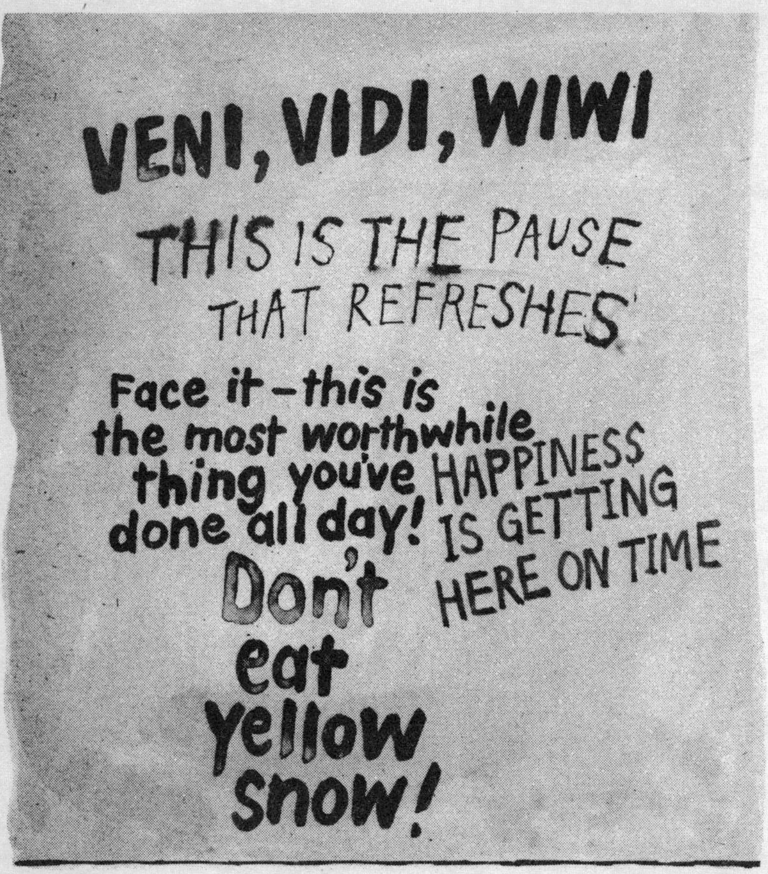
VENI, VIDI, WIWI
THIS IS THE PAUSE THAT REFRESHES
Face it—this is the most worthwhile thing you've done all day!
HAPPINESS IS GETTING HERE ON TIME
Don't eat yellow snow!

99

LITTLE DROPS OF WATER
UPON THE TOILET FLOOR
USES LOTS OF ELBOW GREASE
AND MAKES THE PORTER SORE.

SO NOW, KIND FRIENDS, REMEMBER
BEFORE THE WATER FLOWS
PLEASE ADJUST THE DISTANCE
ACCORDING TO YOUR HOSE.

I used to be
a war artist
but now I'm
just a peace artist

Do not throw
cigarettes in the pissoir.
It makes them soggy
and difficult to light!

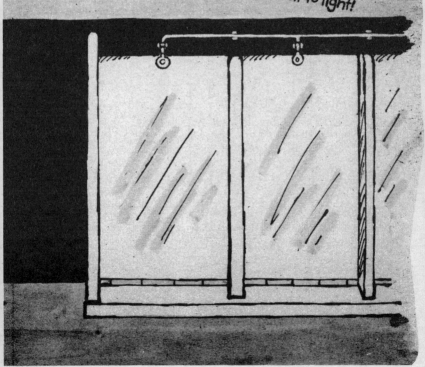

101

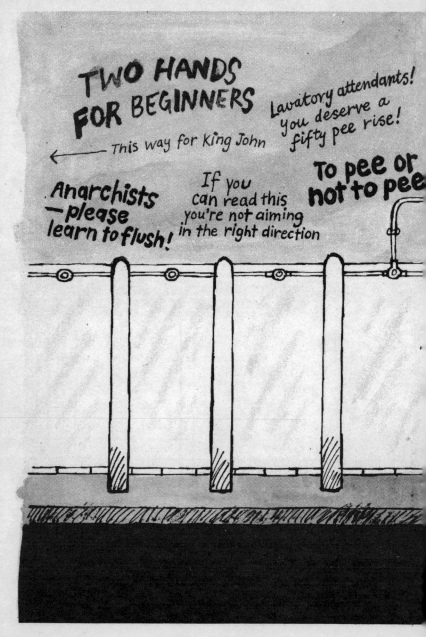

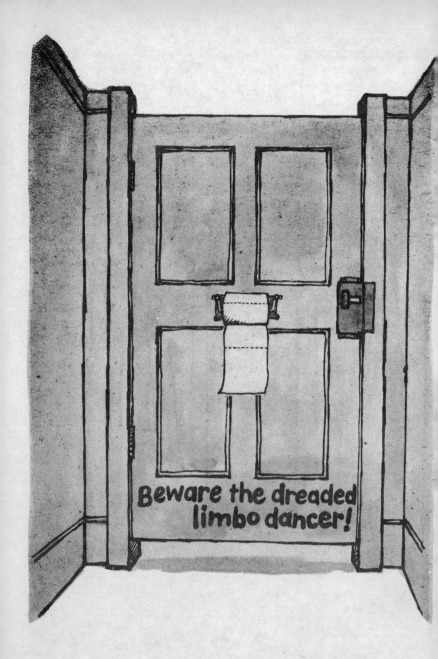

DO NOT
WRITE
ON THE WALL.

You want we
should type maybe?

Write your own
Graffiti

Write your own Graffiti

Write your own
Graffiti

Write your own
Graffiti

Write your own
Graffiti

Write your own Graffiti

Write your own Graffiti

GRAFFITI 2:

The Walls of the World

CONTENTS

WELCOME TO THE WALLS OF THE WORLD

This is Mr McLachlan's and my second collection of global graffiti. Our first — Graffiti, The Scrawl of the Wild (Corgi 1979) — swept the world and enabled us to stop sweeping the streets. It also provoked thousands of letters — well three, to be honest — all asking the same thing. Where can we find the best graffiti for ourselves?

And that question from the three of you has prompted this answer from the two of us: right here. Ladies and gentlemen, boys and girls and the rest of you who are either in between or undecided, Kilroy and McLachlan proudly present the world's first Good Graffiti Guide.

Graffiti hunting is an art and you'll waste time and energy if you don't know the tricks of the trade. So join with us as we penetrate the minds of the wall scribes and lead you to the secret and the not-so-secret places, where they unleash their caustic wisdom on an unsuspecting world.

Come graffiti hunting with the pair of us and you'll not only have a few laughs and come face to face with a few home truths (and rather more half truths), you'll also learn a lot about the true nature of society in the eighties.

For example, in the pages that follow, there is much to cheer the forlorn teacher who is convinced that the young have gone to the dogs — or to the horses, or even to bingo. The walls of our schools and colleges at least show one thing — the young still have plenty to say, even if they can't always spell it 'write'.

In fact whatever your profession, your interest or your bent — because some of our graffiti do seem to be a little queer — you will find great inspiration from the Good Graffiti Guide. Just take your notebook and pencil (and your spray can because the graffiti hunter is really a graffiti writer in disguise) and follow us onto the streets but please not into the loo — that's one place where I still like to do private research.

7

Education kills by degrees!

Graffiti in the classroom:

Desk tops used to be the traditional home of student graffiti. In days gone by any comment banned from the exercise book had a good chance of being inscribed in wood instead. Today's scholars aren't so particular and the modern student is happy to adorn almost anything with his scrawl. If you want to know what the young are thinking, among the best places to look are in the changing rooms, the showers, and the bicycle sheds. Here is a sample from our survey of the world's academic institutions, a modest tribute to youthful wit.

9

THE FRENCH NATIONAL ANTHEM IS THE MAYONNAISE

You have to keep a watch on the Swiss.

MORTALITY IS AN ESSENTIAL PART OF LIFE

Latin is the language of the dead

EUREKA! you're not too fresh yourself

FOR THE MILLIONTH TIME, STOP EXAGGERATING

Bring
back
the
dinosaur

OWING
TO LACK
OF
INTEREST
TOMORROW
HAS BEEN
CANCELLED

this space to let

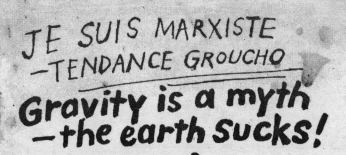

JE SUIS MARXISTE
—TENDANCE GROUCHO

**Gravity is a myth
—the earth sucks!**

Ring around a neutron
A pocket full of protons
A fission, a fusion
We all fall down.

OEDIPUS WAS A NERVOUS REX.

EAT, DRINK AND BE MERRY FOR TOMORROW WE MAY BE RADIOACTIVE

CRY 'HAVOC!' AND LET SLIP THE DOGS OF WAR —AMONGST MY DAD'S PRIZE GERANIUMS!

POPEYE —TELL OLIVE TO GET STUFFED!

Boots, Boots, Boots, Boots, Marching up and down on sir.

The grave of Karl Marx is just another communist plot.

WHEN THE LAST OF THE SOCIOLOGISTS
HAS BEEN STRANGLED WITH THE INTESTINES
OF THE LAST BUREAUCRAT, WILL WE STILL
HAVE PROBLEMS?
ANSWER ON A POSTCARD PLEASE.

100,000 LEMMINGS CAN'T BE WRONG.

PROCRASTINATE NOW!

MATRICULATION MAKES YOU DEAF

The world is flat—

Beware the thundrous trowel surgeons

Class of 1492

BAN UNDERAGE DRINKING

Well, I'm sweet sixteen
and never been pissed.

DO YOU HAVE TROUBLE
IN MAKING UP YOUR MIND?
—well, yes and no.

| TO DO IS TO BE | TO BE IS TO DO | DOBEDOBEDO |
| — Rousseau | —Sartre | —Sinatra |

15

Bruce Lee is not dead
— He's just kicking around somewhere!

A Pessimist is a man who looks after your feet
— NO THAT'S A PEDOPHILE YOU FOOL

RICHARD CŒUR DE LION
— FIRST HEART TRANSPLANT

join the hernia society — it needs your support

17

Business as usual. (Full stop)

Graffiti in the office:

Happiness can't buy money, which is why most of us have to go to work — and many of us find the place where we work is the office, an ideal setting for graffiti, which can be daubed in liquid Tippex or even issued in triplicate . . .

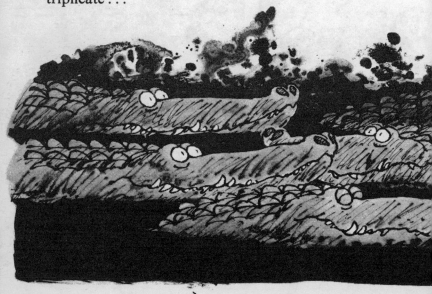

Six munfs ago I cudn't even spel executiv. Now I are wun.

THE OBJECT OF ALL DEDICATED COMPANY EMPLOYEES
SHOULD BE TO ANALYSE THOROUGHLY ALL SITUATIONS;
ANTICIPATE ALL PROBLEMS PRIOR TO THEIR OCCURENCE;
HAVE ANSWERS TO ALL THESE PROBLEMS AND MOVE SWIFTLY
TO SOLVE THESE PROBLEMS WHEN CALLED UPON..
HOWEVER....
WHEN YOU ARE UP TO YOUR ARSE IN ALLIGATORS, IT IS
DIFFICULT TO REMIND YOURSELF THAT YOUR INITIAL
OBJECTIVE WAS TO DRAIN THE SWAMP!

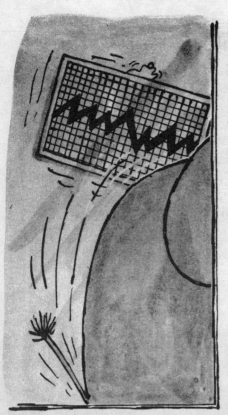

Getting things done around here is like mating elephants!
It's done at high level —
It's accomplished with a great deal of roaring and screaming —
It takes 2 years to produce results!

20

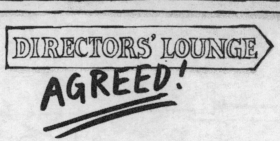

Customers giving orders
will be promptly executed.

THINK
OR THWIM!

The typist's reproduction equipment
is not to be interfered with without prior
permission of the manager

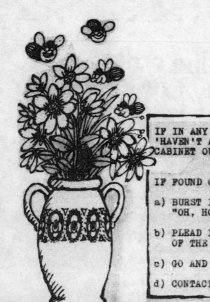

IF IN ANY DOUBT FILE UNDER 'H' FOR
'HAVEN'T A CLUE' AND HURL KEY OF
CABINET OUT OF NEAREST WINDOW.

IF FOUND OUT:

a) BURST INTO TEARS SOBBING
   "OH, HOW COULD YOU...etc".

b) PLEAD INSANITY AND ASK FOR THE REST
   OF THE DAY OFF.

c) GO AND LOOK FOR THE KEY.

d) CONTACT INDUSTRIAL TRIBUNAL.

IN BRIGHTON SHE WAS BRIDGET
SHE WAS PATSY UP IN PERTH
IN CAMBRIDGE SHE WAS CLARISSA
THE GRANDEST GIRL ON EARTH:
IN STAFFORD SHE WAS STELLA.
THE BEST OF ALL THE BUNCH,
BUT DOWN ON HIS EXPENSE ACCOUNT
SHE WAS PETROL, OIL AND LUNCH.

A specialist is someone brought in at the last minute to share the blame.

MY BOSS HAS BOOTS SO SHINY I CAN SEE MY FACE IN THEM

YOU CAN FOOL SOME OF THE PEOPLE ALL OF THE TIME AND ALL OF THE PEOPLE SOME OF THE TIME. A COMBINATION OF WHICH KEEPS THIS COMPANY GOING!

MUSHROOM MANAGEMENT —KEEP YOUR EMPLOYEES IN THE DARK AND OCCASIONALLY THROW CHIT AT THEM

GENERAL OFFICE

CHIT

The wages of sin is death but the wages here are worse

27

The first 90% of the task
takes 10% of the time and
the last 10% takes
the other 90%

Gather
up as much
paperwork
as possible
and run
towards
the flames

PLENTY
OF WASTE
PAPER
IN
FUTURE
PROJECTS FILE

A lovely
way to
drown

Keep Britain tidy —Kill a tourist!

Graffiti in poster paradise:

Some signs of the times need no adornment . . .

'DUE TO INDUSTRIAL ACTION ALL GRAVE DIGGING THIS WEEK WILL BE UNDERTAKEN BY A SKELETON CREW' — notice in a Norfolk cemetery.

'OUR CURRIES ARE SO DELICIOUS, YOU WILL REPEAT OFTEN!' — advertisement in a Manchester restaurant.

'SINCE WE ARE ANXIOUS TO MAINTAIN A HIGH STANDARD OF SERVICE TO OUR CUSTOMERS, THIS BRANCH WILL BE CLOSED ALL DAY ON WEDNESDAYS AND THURSDAYS' — sign in a shop window in London.

. . . but others don't stand on their own so effectively. In fact, most posters can be improved with a touch of well-placed graffiti . . .

31

What will you do when this silicon chip learns your job?
—Make-one-that-can do yours
Marry it, of course!

JOIN THE ARMY. MEET INTERESTING PEOPLE—AND KILL THEM!

HARWICH FOR THE CONTINENT!
Frinton for the Incontinent!

CRYSTAL PALACE F.C. - TOMORROW'S TEAM, TODAY!

Ah, but that was yesterday

Send our athletes to MOSCOW

AND OUR POLITICIANS TO SIBERIA!

BUS STOP

IT'S 85 IN JAMAICA RIGHT NOW WHAT ARE YOU WAITING FOR?

ANY BUS TO BRIXTON

JAMAICA

SAVE TREES - EAT A BEAVER!

FAMILY TEA BREEDS CONTEMPT

Flying is still the safest way to fly

I've had a spaniel in my works

P.-P-P- PICK UP A PENGUIN
— AND SMACK ITS HEAD AGAINST A WALL
SMITHFIELD MARKET
DO NOT FEED THE ANIMALS. THEY ARE DEAD.
Meat me under the clock
Old accountants never die - They just lose their balance.
P.G. LIVIN-DEADE
Vindaloo purges the parts other curries cannot reach

BUT THE LADY DOESN'T LIKE MILK TRAY!!
Move up to a Colt
I'D RATHER MOUNT A FILLY!
SIGMA
Move up to a
COLT
MITSUBISHI MOTORS CORP.
COLT
GITTERIDGE & GUNNS
FUNERAL DIRECTORS
YOU-KILL'EM-
-WE CHILL'EM!
ICE
BUY BLITISH!

Come to the
bank of IRELAND
28 SOUTH ALBION ST. DONCASTER MAY 17/81

KEY UNDER THE MAT!

HEAT N'EAT

CHICKEN & HAM PIE
with finely pastry nit

A meal in minutes!

BE ALERT

YOUR COUNTRY NEEDS LERTS

FAST FOOD MAKES YOU SICK QUICK!

Keep Reggae white
HOMES BEFORE OFFICES. PEOPLE BEFORE CARS.
LEG BEFORE WICKET
My Parrot's dead —That's Life!
FIGHT WORLD HUNGER -Feed the Iranians to the cambodians!
RACIAL PREJUDICE IS A PIGMENT OF THE IMAGINATION
WET PAINT
This is not an instruction!

BELFAST WILL TAKE YOUR BREATH AWAY
—PERMANENTLY—

EAST LANE
TRAVEL BUREAU
629, PARTINGTON HIGH STREET, PELHAM TEL 20012/3301

Visit the Soviet Union
—before the
Soviet Union
visits you !!

When theres no more
room in HELL
the dead will walk
the EARTH

ZOMBIES
DAWN OF THE DEAD (X)

A FILM
ABOUT
CHARTERED
ACCOUNTANTS

Bad news – Good God

Graffiti in the place of God:

God moves in mysterious ways his
wonders to perform.

Man is much more obvious
and if proof is what you're after,
here it is: graffiti (sacred and profane)
from the priest,
the pagan
and the penitent.

43

44

God uses Vox amplifiers

Down with early Byzantine Church music.

RELIGION IS THE OPIUM OF THE CONGREGATIONZZZZZZZZ

GOD—I SUSPECT YOU OF BEING A LEFT-WING INTELLECTUAL

A MAN'S BEST FRIEND IS HIS DOGMA

GOD WAS A WOMAN — UNTIL SHE CHANGED HER MIND

J.C. LOVES M.E.

It's no good trying to put spilt milk back into the bottle

Religion is man's attempt to communicate with the weather.

REINCARNATION IS A PLEASANT SURPRISE.

Work for the Lord — The pay is terrible but the fringe benefits are out of this world!

46

CHURCH OF Sͭ BARTHOLEMEW

ARE YOU TIRED OF SIN AND LONGING FOR A REST?

IF NOT, PHONE BAYSWATER 81762

Where will you be on the Day of Judgement?

STILL HERE, WAITING FOR A 31 BUS!

SUFFER LITTLE CHILDREN

Especially those with transistor radios !!!

And the angel of the
Lord said unto the shepherds
"Shove off, this is cattle country!"
Don't blame God -he's only human
Blessed are the meek for they shall inhibit the earth

THE POPE LIVES IN A VACUUM

Jews are like
everyone else
—only more so!

CHRIST DID NOT SAY
—'KILL TREES FOR CHRISTMAS'
Jog for Jesus

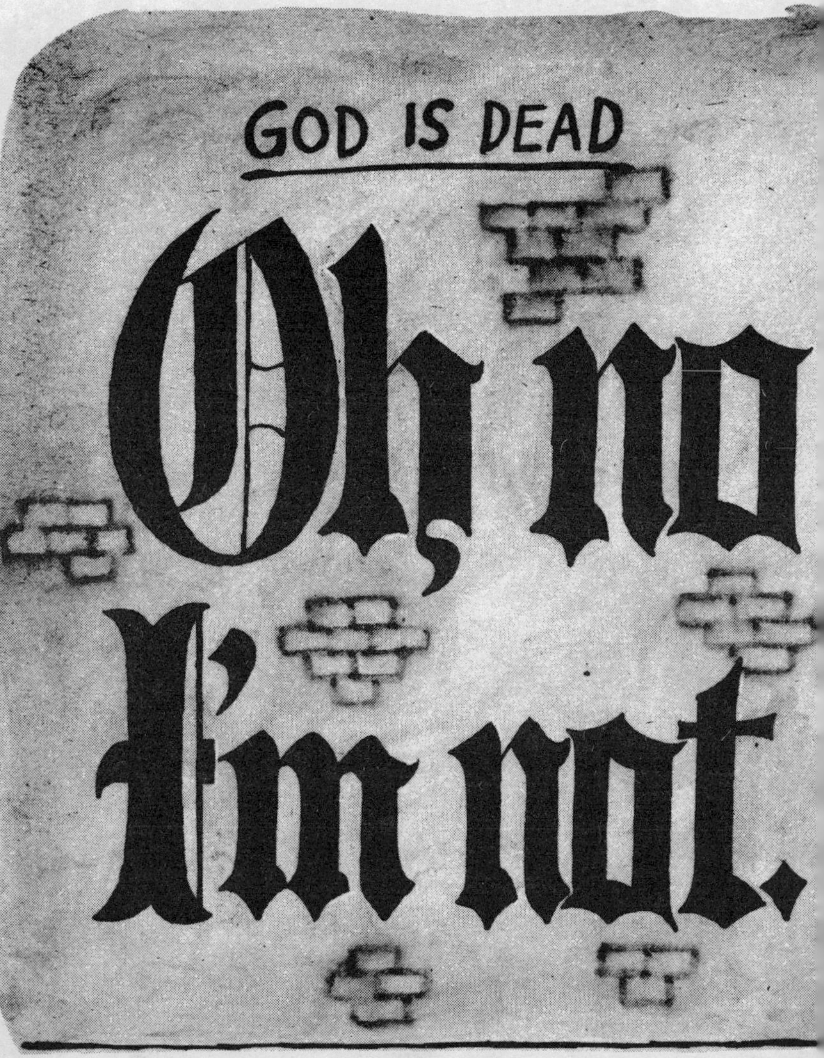
GOD IS DEAD
Oh no
I'm not.

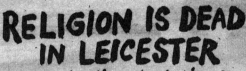

RELIGION IS DEAD
IN LEICESTER
— so *that's* what the smell is!

GOD IS NOT DEAD,
BUT ALIVE AND WELL
AND WORKING ON
A MUCH LESS
AMBITIOUS PROJECT.

JESUS
SAVES

First
Division
championship
for
Man.
United

JESUS
SAVES

— But
Shilton
is
Better

Freedom for all —What's yours is mine and what's mine is my own!

Graffiti where squatters dwell:

Anyone who is bumming around in search of the Sixties is liable to end up squatting—literally. And a deserted house is not only a squatter's paradise—its large bare walls make ideal canvases for the graffiti guru yearning to express the voice of the alternative society. To bring you what follows, and purely in the interests of literary research, of course, we join the passing out parade . . .

53

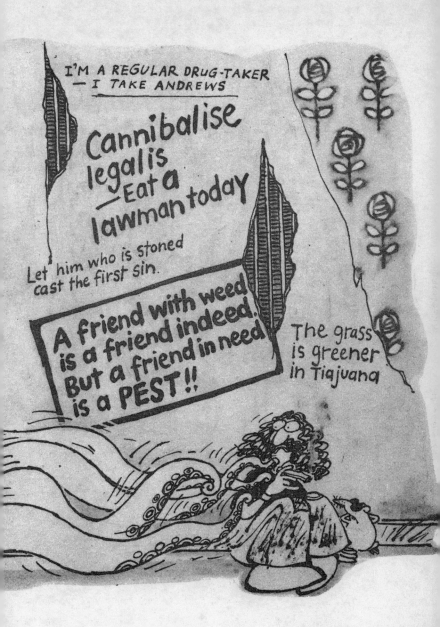

RIGHT ON
Left off
Right UP
LEFT OUT
Right wing
LEFT LEG
RIGHT IN
Left back
Right Boring

HERE WE SQUAT
& HERE WE STAY

FRUZZTRATE
THE FUZZ

I hate graffiti
— Dirty rats, they killed my brother!

Graffiti behind prison bars:

If you are doing time you have time—so unlike the poster graffitist who may have to scribble and scrawl at speed as the train starts to pull out of the station, the prison inmate can be as patient and painstaking in his work as he wants. You will find prison graffiti etched on the cutlery, embroidered on mailbags, carved into re-enforced concrete and even tatooed about a prisoner's person. These examples come from the inside, finally proving our total dedication to the task . . .

59

Humpty Dumpty
was pushed

MY WIFE HAD HAD THE CHANGE OF LIFE
SO I THOUGHT I'D HAVE A CHANGE OF WIFE
— AND NOW THEY'VE SENT ME DOWN FOR LIFE

Free the Heinz 57

Free Chile!
NO THANKS, HONEY, I'SE ALREADY GOT ONE

FREE GEORGE DAVIS
— WITH EVERY PACKET
OF CORNFLAKES

If Jesus saves
he must be
working a
tax fiddle

61

I WAS IN REFUSE DISPOSAL IN BELFAST
— DISPOSING OF THOSE WHO REFUSE!

Don't make a fool out
of me — I'm doing OK by myself!

GIVE A MAN
ENOUGH ROPE
AND HE'LL HANG YOU

Hanging concentrates
the mind wonderfully
IT ALSO CURES CONSTIPATION

We are all
under control

I AM HERE BECAUSE I'M AN ARSIST

surely you mean 'arsonist.'

I KNOW WHAT I MEAN, <u>DUCKIE</u>!

Three-channel TV sets – Guaranteed perfect working order – As advertised on 'POLICE 5'

Evil spelt backwards is live

Don't burn your bridges until you come to them.

A rat's a rat for a' that!

WE'LL HAVE PEACE IN ULSTER IF WE HAVE TO KILL EVERYONE TO DO IT.

YOU HAVE TO TAKE THE BAD WITH THE <u>WORST</u>

Poetry is when every line begins with a capita.

Graffiti behind the library shelves:

If you need answers to the burning literary
questions of the day—

> Was Oscar Wilde?
> Was Thornton Wilder?
> Can Alastair Cooke?
> What the Dickens?

—the man to turn to is McLachlan.
When he was a lad, his father used to take him to
school every day. He had to, poor soul: they were in
the same class. Neither of them learnt much there, but
they spent many happy and fulfilling hours in the
school library and there they discovered a good deal—
much of it now revealed for the first time on the next
few pages . . .

SHAKESPEARE
BRINGS HOME
THE BACON

Words mean
nothing today!

T.S. Eliot is an
anagram of
Toilets

Tolkien is
Hobbit-forming

TOLKIEN   The only
SPOKIEN   good
           books
HERE   are read
           ones

Frodo has
been busted!

Mozambique is full of black Marx.

HERMAN MELVILLE EATS BLUBBER

Henry James must have f**cked somebody

I wandered lonely as a cloud because I had B.O.

SEXTON BLAKE LOVES TO HAVE A TINKER

It's a good job that William Ewart Gladstone is dead. He's been buried an awful long time!

MOUNTAINEERING

Agatha Christie
has died—
Whodunnit?

Who will rid
me of this
turbulent Proust?

**BEDE
THRILLS**

MR KIPLING WRITES
EXCEEDINGLY
GOOD BOOKS

Back in a
minute—Godot

MOBY
DICK IS
A HONKY

Insanity is hereditary —You get it from your kids!

Graffiti by the psychiatrist's couch:

If you ever felt you were just a pair of curtains, pull yourself together. And concentrate. What you are about to receive are graffiti from the minds of the lunatic, the paranoid and the manic-depressive — and they're just the shrinks. What their loopy patients have to say is almost as disturbing. However, all insanity is relative (as anyone with a crazy old aunt will tell you), we do live in a mad, mad world, and you're only Jung once, so stop twitching and read on . . .

PSYCHOLOGY IS PRODUCING HABITS OUT OF A RAT

There's no problem so big and complicated that it can't be run away from.

HAPPINESS IS MELANCHOLOGY

You can observe a lot by watching.

Life is just a bowl of toenails

MOON JUNE SPOON LOON

72

SURREY HAS A LUNATIC FRINGE ON TOP!

I wish I were
what I was when
I wished I were what I am.

NECESSITY IS THE MOTHER OF CONVENTION

Lead in the atmosphere can affect one's I.Q. — especially if it drops on one's head.

When you talk to me — SHUT UP!

IS THERE LIFE BEFORE DEATH?

Going to a psychiatrist didn't cure my drink problem — I kept falling off the couch!

HOME IS WHERE YOU HANG YOUR HEAD

SADISM —THE SCIENCE OF BEING UNHAPPY?

Let's get down to the brass roots.

How happy is the moron,
He doesn't give a damn.
I wish I were a moron,
My God, perhaps I am!

74

I either want less corruption—or more chance to participate in it!

Graffiti in the red-light district:

The committed student of graffiti must be prepared to risk both life and limb—or at least infection and arrest—in his relentless pursuit of the ultimate in wall-talk. If you want to join us as we snoop around the lurid red-light districts of the world, you must be prepared to find yourself in a compromising position—but what is art without suffering?

I USED TO HAVE MONEY
TO BURN — AND MY LOVER
WAS THE BEST MATCH.

Does oral sex mean just
talking about it?

You're a better man
than I, Mrs Dinn — Gunga

A CIGAR IS ONLY
A CIGAR BUT A
GOOD WOMAN IS A POKE

MARY HAD A LITTLE LAMB
WITH WHICH SHE USED TO SLEEP
TOO LATE SHE FOUND IT WAS A RAM
AND NOW SHE HAS A LITTLE LAMB

WHO SCREWED
LOO BY LOO?
— ANDY RANDY!

Repeal Inhibition!!

Absinthe makes the tart grow fonder

Once I was a love-child Now I'm just a little bastard

A LITTLE YEARNING IS A DANGEROUS THING

Someone, somewhere wants some heavy breathing from you.

AND HOW DID YOU FIND YOURSELF THIS MORNING? I JUST ROLLED BACK THE SHEETS AND THERE I WAS.

WOMEN TEND TO GET ALL JUMPY DURING THEIR MINSTREL PERIODS

If jewellery is a collection of jewels, flattery is a collection of flats and pantry is a collection of pants then what is coquetry?

WOMEN LIKE THE SIMPLER THINGS IN LIFE - LIKE MEN

Avant-Garde.
— a French chastity belt

I THOUGHT CLAP
WAS A FORM OF APPLAUSE
UNTIL I DISCOVERED SMIRNOFF

Support
Women's Lib–Make
him sleep in
the wet patch

STERILITY
IS
HERIDITARY

my sister
uses
massacre
on her eyes

Snow White
thought 7-up was
a soft drink until
she discovered
Smirnoff

DOES THE LATERAL COITAL POSITION
MEAN HAVING A BIT ON THE SIDE?

UNDERNEATH
THOSE SHABBY
TROUSERS BEATS
A HEART OF GOLD

CUNNILINGUS
SPOKEN
HERE

VIDI VICI VENI

85

Time in loo –Take a holiday – Let your trousers down!

Graffiti in convenient places:

Once the champagne has flowed freely—or the beer has been downed—even the most upright colonel, the most refined aristocrat, the most straight-laced matron, the most sophisticated girl-about-town can be overwhelmed with an irresistable urge to scribble on convenient walls. Everyone in the world goes to the loo now and again (and again and again and again) and everyone has something to say . . .

89

My Dad says they don't work

Since writing on lavatory walls is done neither for personal acclaim nor financial reward, it must be the purest form of art.

Discuss.

GRAFFITI 3:

The Golden Graffiti Awards

CONTENTS

Page

Life is a tragedy — we're here today and tomorrow.

The Most Profound Graffiti Award:

Graffiti writers are philosophers. They contemplate the human condition. They realise that a slight inclination of the cranium is as adequate as a spasmodic movement of one optic to an equine quadruped utterly devoid of any visionary capacity and consequently use the visual loud-hailer of the blank wall to communicate to the rest of humanity their own understanding of life in all its aspects.

If you didn't understand a word of that, read on . . . (If you did, you've bought the wrong book.)

8

TWO CAN LIVE
AS CHEAPLY AS ONE
– FOR HALF AS LONG

Mother Nature is a bitch

LAUGH, AND THE WORLD THINKS YOU'RE AN IDIOT

Every day is the dawn of a new error.

Just when I was getting used to yesterday along came today.

If you can only talk ill of people— come and sit by me.

EVERY MAN REAPS WHAT HE SOWS —except the amateur gardener!

on't
get mad
-get even!!

Laugh, and the
world laughs with you
— SNORE, AND YOU SLEEP ALONE!!

Where there's
a will — there's
a greedy
solicitor getting
in on the act.

HOW COME IT'S
NEVER THE
COLD GIRL WHO
GETS THE FUR COAT?

ALL THAT GLITTERS IS NOT GOLD
All that doesn't glitter isn't either

SHOPLIFTERS HAVE
THE GIFT OF THE GRAB!

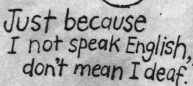

Just because
I not speak English,
don't mean I deaf.

I get on
with everyone
— except humans
and Tories!!

WHAT
DID WE DO
BEFORE
NOSTALGIA?

SMILE — THINGS
MAY GET WORSE
MORE SLOWLY

GOD
BLESS
ATHEISM!

14

15

17

Beware of the doc.

The Healthiest Hospital Graffiti Award:

In hospital Doctors and Nurses scribble graffiti on charts at the ends of beds to take their minds off each other and to help preserve their patients. As you'll see from what follows, graffiti doesn't need an Arts Council grant while it has the National Health Service.

When you're healthy
you walk tall.
- When you've piles
you sit tall

I'M SCHIZOPHRENIC
That makes four of us!

s having hysterics
a kind of sick joke?

'M HAVING
ROUBLE WITH
MY BREATHING
Get something
to stop it!

I FEEL LIKE
A NEW WOMAN
AND I ONLY CAME IN
TO HAVE MY
PROSTATE REMOVED.

Gynaecologists put in a hard day at the orifice.

I NEED HELP. IN BEING ABLE TO ADMIT I NEED HELP.

I'D RATHER HAVE A FULL BOTTLE IN FRONT OF ME THAN A FULL FRONTAL LOBOTOMY!

You need Help!!

IS ARTIFICIAL INSEMINATION THE INNOCULATE CONCEPTION?

I could live a better life if I had a better body.

HELP! I'M A PAUPER! Congratulations. Boy or girl?

IF YOU'D LIVED A BETTER LIFE YOU MIGHT HAVE HAD A BETTER BODY!

DEATH IS HERIDITARY

O.K. I'M CURED OF SCHIZOPHRENIA
BUT WHERE WILL I BE
WHEN I NEED ME?

No Nurse!
I said 'Remove his
spectacles and
prick his boil!'

I don't mind the pain
- it proves I'm alive!

Constipation is the thief of time
DIARRHOEA WAITS FOR NO MAN

Avoid life - it'll kill you
in the end

THE WAY DOCS INJECT THEIR FLOCKS
SMALL WONDER THEIR PATIENTS FEAR 'EM.
THE CURE PRODUCES BURNS AND SHOCKS;
THEY DON'T JUST PRICK, THEY SERUM.

Am I still alive?

Trying to relax is a great strain on my nerves.

ACCEPT ME FOR
WHAT I AM —SICK!

It'll never
heal if
you picket.

I USED TO BE A WEREWOLF
—BUT I'M ALL RIGHT NOWWWWWWWH!

Is there an imaginary cure for hypochondria?
I've got too much blood in my alcohol stream.
HIC!
WASH YOUR NECK -I'M A VAMPIRE
Go gay-It means not having a vasectomy
VASECTOMY MEANS NOT HAVING TO SAY YOU'RE SORRY.
HYPOCHONDRIA KILLS -O.K? Eventually

I hope I don't die before they find a cure....

My surgeon must hate me — he keeps sticking the knife in.

RICKETS, LOVELY RICKETS — IT WAS AT LOUDRES WHERE I SAW THEM.

Uncle Alf died of asbestiosis — It took six months to cremate him!

OPERATIONS ARE FUNNY — THEY HAVE YOU IN STITCHES.

SLEEPING PILLS ARE NOD ADDICTIVE

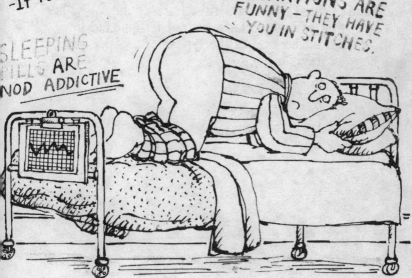

27

To err is human – to totally muck things up needs a computer.

The Least Oafish Office Graffiti Award:

Wherever you work, the graffitist works too. At every level of industry, from the basement garage to the roof-top boardroom, from the factory floor to the executive toilet, great graffiti can be found. Whether it is posing as an official memo or is tippexed in shorthand on the side of the typewriter, office graffiti is here to stay.

Being employed here is like making love to a hedgehog — one prick against thousands!

INCOMES POLICY HERE IS ABOUT AS SIGNIFICANT AS A BLUSH ON A DEAD MAN'S CHEEK

Always put the important before the merely urgent!

God has mercifully withheld from man the fore-knowledge of what will sell.

It's like Treasure Island here — Fifteen men on a good man's back.

WHEN IN DOUBT — MUMBLE.

ALWAYS BE SINCERE — EVEN WHEN YOU DON'T MEAN IT

Work is the lowest hierarchal level in any human enterprise.

I'm much too busy here to do any work

NEVER PUT OFF TO TOMORROW WHAT YOU CAN AVOID ALTOGETHER

IS COMPUTERISED GOSSIP JUST MICRO-CHIP-CHAT?

WHEN IN TROUBLE - DELEGATE

THE ROAD TO SUCCESS IS USUALLY UNDER CONSTRUCTION

Things are not nearly
as bad as they seem.
NO, THEY'RE A BLOODY
SIGHT WORSE!!

WHAT HAS THE BOSS
GOT THAT I HAVEN'T
How did he get it?

The union is my shepherd;
I shall not work

LORD GIVE ME PATIENCE
BUT HURRY!
She's my favourite typist too!

The work is hard
The pay is small.
So take your time
And sod 'em all.

32

Doing a good job here is like
wetting your pants in a dark suit;
You get a warm feeling but nobody notices.

**EMPLOYEES ASK FOR A SALARY
INCREASE AT THEIR OWN RISK**

THE MONEY
THAT MEN
MAKE
LIVES
AFTER
THEM.

Where there's
a will there's
an inheritance
tax!

Everyone has
a right to my
own opinion.

33

34

THE LAW OF INCREASING IMPORTANCE
AN EXECUTIVE'S IMPORTANCE IS PROPORTIONAL TO THE
DISTANCE FROM HIS OFFICE DOOR TO THE DESK IN FEET,
MULTIPLIED BY THE THICKNESS OF HIS OFFICE CARPET
IN CENTIMETRES.

THE KISS-OF-DEATH LAW
THE LIKELIHOOD OF WHAT APPEARS TO BE A WISE AND
IMPRESSIVE STATEMENT OF FACT BEING REVERSED BY
NATURE ALMOST IMMEDIATELY IT IS MADE, IS ENHANCED
BY THE IMPORTANCE OF THE SPEAKER.

GLORIA, I LOVE YOU,
I WANT YOU, I WOULD
DIE FOR YOU, GO THROUGH
FIRE FOR YOU, CLIMB MOUNTAINS
FOR YOU, SWIM OCEANS FOR YOU.

See you Saturday
—If it isn't raining /G.

When all else fails, scream!

DON'T PANIC —COUNT TO TEN Then panic!!

35

Help the police—beat yourself up.

The Very Important Poster Graffiti Award:

All around us are billboards, hoardings and posters
featuring advertisements and announcements of every
kind. Sometimes they inform us, sometimes they
infuriate us, very rarely do they entertain us—that
is, unless the graffitist has been around. Take a look
at the choice signs of the times...

37

38

Don't let anxiety kill you
— Allow the Church to help.

A phone call costs less than you think

SOON IT'LL COST MORE THAN YOU BELIEVE!

BUZBY

Make someone happy.
STUFF BUZBY FOR XMAS?

H
THE HARBOROUGH PLAYERS
PRESENT

HAMLET
Son of Piglet

BY
WILLIAM SHAKESPEARE

STARTING JUNE 6TH - 30TH
TICKETS AVAILABLE AT OFFICES

SEATS £1 - £1.50 — SHOW 7.30

walls have ears
— So be careful what you say
especially about their sausages!

← This way to the creche
— THERE'S BEEN AN ACCIDENT IN KENSINGTON

The Annual Conference of Clairvoyants has been cancelled due to unforeseen circumstances.

The DUBLIN SAMARITANS are ex-directory.

LAST TUESDAY'S MEETING OF THE APATHY SOCIETY HAS BEEN CANCELLED —
— So what?

THE SCOTS SUPPLY THE POETRY
THE IRISH SUPPLY THE PROSE
THE WELSH SUPPLY THE MUSIC
THE ENGLISH SUPPLY THE AUDIENCE

41

43

Join the Army and see the ^{NEXT} world.

Join the Army and see the ^NEXT world.

The Army will make you a man!

Will it make me one
— six foot tall
with a hairy chest
— Emma Bulstrode
(Miss)

The Army

Drop in on your local SAS office — before they drop in on you!

COULD YOU LEAD A 30 MAN COMMANDO RAID ON AN ENEMY BEACH AT NIGHT?

Ask for information at local office

ROYAL MARINES OFFICERS

Join the professionals

AND LEARN TO KILL WHILE BEING PAID FOR IT!!

REMEMBER CLACTON SEAFRONT
SUMMER OF 1978!
— EAST END BOOT BOYS

It's a man's life in the British Army
— but an Afghan's life in the Russian Army!

44

SAVE ENERGY!
BE CREMATED WITH A FRIEND!
Stand in the dole queue <u>quietly</u>.
Make Love slowly!

Be apathetic today
 — I THINK I'LL LEAVE IT
       UNTIL TOMORROW.

45

Corporal punishment smacks of sadism.

The Wurst Un-Akaddemic Graffiti Award:

Schools, colleges and universities have long been responsible for some of the most imaginative and illuminating of all wall-wisdom. Of course graffitists are getting younger all the time and it won't be long before a playpen isn't a wooden cage for toddlers but a writing implement for pre-teen scribes.

47

49

Little Women
become Very Big Women
—You should see my Mum!

God is black
YES, SHE IS !!

ISAAC NEWTON WAS RIGHT
—THIS IS THE CENTRE OF GRAVITY.

TOILETS

Katy did it
for kicks

Go to
university
—Be the most
qualified
in the dole queue

Examinations
—Nature's Laxative

90% OF HEADMASTERS TAKE "THE GUARDIAN"
—THE OTHER 10% BUY IT!

WHERE'S THE BLOODY CHALK THEN?

Forty Years On —and this bloody place might have fallen down by then.

SCHOOL DINNERS ARE GOING UP AGAIN —THEY'RE VERY HARD TO KEEP DOWN!

52

BIGGLES FLIES OPEN

I LEARNED TO PLAY THE TRUMPET AT 84
must have been hell for those
living at 82 and 86.

HAVE YOU READ THE
PENGUIN BOOK OF
QUOTATIONS?
I never realised
penguins had that
much to say

KEEP LONDON
TIDY
—EAT A PIGEON

Noah's Ark is bigger than Joan's.

The Popular Personality Graffiti Award:

You may meet the Queen, you may appear on
Desert Island Discs and *This Is Your Life*, you may
be given the Freedom of the City of London and a
seat in the House of Lords, but you haven't really
arrived until you've been scrawled on a wall.
Immortality is when your friends tell you you're a
brick—and it's true!

Ronald Reagan
doesn't dye his hair
—He's just prematurely orange!

RICHARD
thE ZIONHear†
was the first
king of ISRAEL

Yorick is a numbSKULL!

DAILY NEWS

MORE
RUSSIAN
SETBACKS
IN
AFGHANISTAN
If this is world
domination, you can
stuff it *private Ivanov*

Vandyke
was a
lesbian
truck driver

LORD
LUCAN
IS ALIVE
AND WELL
AND LIVING
IN SLOUGH

He can't be
well then

56

MARY WHITEHOUSE IS AN ANGEL
She bloody well ought to be!

MAGGIE THATCHER SHOULD GO INTO POLITICS

Annie Walker for QUEEN

NOAH'S ARK WAS BIGGER THAN JOAN'S
But Joan's was maid of orleans

I'm off my head
charles I

Isn't it great to have Reagan as President
—A real actor after all these clowns

AND I'M A KING CHARLES SPANIEL

HELL HATH NO FURY
LIKE A PRIME MINISTER SCORNED
— M. Thatcher

I wouldn't bet on that!
signed 3 million unemployed

CAN ALISTAIR COOKE?
DID EZRA POUND?
DOES SAUL BELLOW?

Shirley Bassey
Sings
— 0000.K Big Spender

Adam was
rejected for
Eden the apple.

Destry Rides
Again — Why?

Magnus Pyke
reaches parts
David Bellamy cannot reach.

BERNARD MANNING HAS
PARTS IN PLACES WHERE OTHER
PEOPLE HAVEN'T EVEN GOT PLACES.

Thought for food.

The Most Edifying Restaurant Graffiti Award:

Eating establishments throughout the world have long been a valuable sauce/source of graffiti. While waiting to be served, we impatient diners put pencil to napkins or write with soup on the tablecloth. And of course we only have to wait so long because the staff are so busy scribbling on the walls in the kitchen . . .

MY WAITER IS HOMOSEXUAL
—Tray Gay!

We're only open to tell you we're closed

THIS RESTAURANT HAS THE
BEST TARTS IN SOHO — Thanks, dearie

I love
children
BOILED OR FRIED?

Goblin your food is bad for your elf.

CAN YOU
HELP ME OUT?

Which way did
you come in?

Ecstasy is a warm codpiece
– I prefer plaice myself
If you eat chicken here, you're no coward!
I like brains
Salome
FAGGOTS RULE
–O. GAY?
BRAINS ARE OFF!
John the Baptist

I've just been to McDonalds
— They're still getting revenge for
the Massacre of Glencoe!

A Restaurant after my
own heart — CESAR BORGIA

Watch out for the
hidden extras at
this restaurant:—
botulism
salmonella
gastro-enteritis

THE WAITER HAS
SHAKY HANDS
— I'VE GOT SOUP
IN MY FLY!

THE LUNCHPACK
OF NOTRE DAME
EATS HERE
— HE'S A SANDWICH MAN!

EAT PRUNES AND FIGS
– THE WORLD WILL FALL
OUT OF YOUR BOTTOM

There are <u>no</u> cockroaches her
–THE RATS HAVE EATEN THEM

You've seen the
show: NOW eat
the pies –Sweeney
Todd

The water
in this
establishment
has been
personally
passed
by the
manager

GENTLEMEN

The prices in this
restaurant merely
keep pace with
inflation.
–IN <u>ARGENTINA</u>

I hate the waitress
- WELL, JUST EAT THE CHIPS & PEAS
You must try the smoked salmonella
DON'T SEND YOUR COMPLIMENTS TO THE CHEF - HE DOESN'T LIKE SARCASM
KITCHEN
IS THIS THE FACE THAT SHIPPED A THOUSAND LUNCHES?
VENI VIDI VOMITI

A miss is as good as a male.

The Best Ladies Graffiti Award:

Queen Victoria would not have believed it, but women do do it—and in the Ladies too! In fact some of the female graffiti that follows was actually found in the women's convenience at Victoria Station. Whatever else they are, the Graffiti Awards are not sexist. We firmly believe in women's writes . . .

I've got one thing
in common with my husband
—We married on the same day!

I'VE GOT TWO THINGS IN
COMMON WITH MINE
—HE DOESN'T LIKE ME,
AND I HATE HIM!

Love is blind
—and when you
get married you
get your eyesight back

Support
Women's Lib
—use his razor.

I
HATE
YOUR LOUSY
GUTS YOU DIRTY
DRUNKEN FOULFACED
LOUDMOUTHED SWEATY
OLD POX DOCTOR'S CLERK!

WOMEN WERE BORN
WITHOUT A SENSE OF
HUMOUR SO THAT THEY
COULD LOVE MEN AND
NOT LAUGH AT THEM.

69

ALL'S FEAR IN LOVE AND WAR.

A penny saved is ridiculous

The bigger they are the harder they maul.

UNDERNEATH EVERY SUCCESSFUL MAN THERE IS A WOMAN

RUTH IS STRANGER THAN FICTION

Where there's a pill, there's a way.

TRANSVESTITES FOOL — O.K.?

Be chairy —or, you'll find you're sitting on a pouffe!

When God made man she was only testing.

DO YOU LIKE MASKED BALLS? No, I like to know who I'm sleeping with.

LAY OFF THE PILL AND LET NATURE TAKE ITS CURSE

I can speak 12 languages —and can't say no in any of them!

I'M A LESBIAN How are things in Beirut then?

Beneath a rough exterior often beats a harlot of gold

IF YOU CAN'T SAY IT TO HIS FACE, SAY IT BEHIND HIS BACK.

CHASTE MAKES WASTE

GET THE ABBEY HABIT —sleep with a monk

Women over 40 needn't worry
about the menopause.
—WORRY ABOUT THE MEN WHO DON'T!

DO MEN CALL US BIRDS BECAUSE WE PICK UP WORMS

BEHIND EVERY
GREAT WOMAN THERE'S
A MAN WHO TRIED
TO STOP HER

I LIKE IT AND
HIM —IN THAT
ORDER!

A seven day
honeymoon makes
one weak.

Has anyone got a contradictive pill?

You're ignorant!

Yes, six months!!

AN
ORGASM
IS A
GLAND FINALE!

I've lost my virginity
HAVE YOU STILL GOT THE RECEIPT?

It's the cow that gives the milk – so why does the bull get all the credit?

IT'S HARD TO BE GOOD
It has to be hard to be good!

A man must do something to relieve the monogamy.

The Best Gents Graffiti Award:

There once was a fellow named Rafferty
Who went to a gentleman's laffertry.
    When he saw the sight
    He said 'Newton was right,
This must be the centre of grafferty.'

This can be no doubt about it—the cradle of graffiti
is the Gents...

JULIAN SUCKS
ORANGES
I am perfectly well adjusted - Do not fiddle with my knob.
I'm gay and Irish - I go out with girls.
Nowadays Bachelors must insert their masculinity

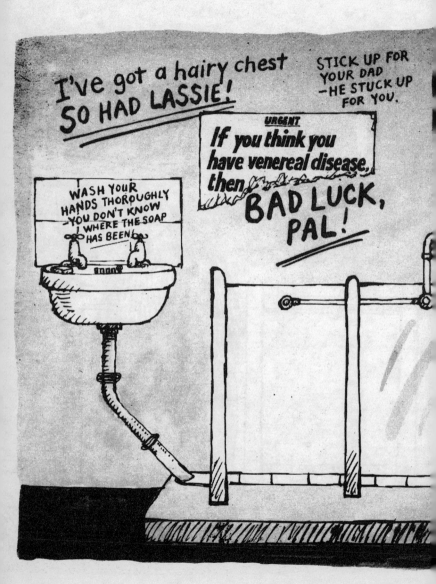

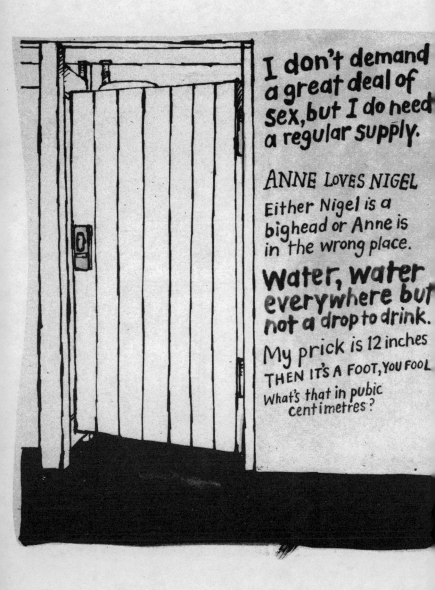

I don't demand a great deal of sex, but I do need a regular supply.

ANNE LOVES NIGEL
Either Nigel is a bighead or Anne is in the wrong place.

Water, water everywhere but not a drop to drink.

My prick is 12 inches
THEN IT'S A FOOT, YOU FOOL
What's that in pubic centimetres?

All the world loves a four-letter word.

The Naughtiest Graffiti Award:

From now on things can only get worse. If you are squeamish, of a nervous disposition, believe in censorship, and always undress in the dark—this sexion is not for you.

87

89

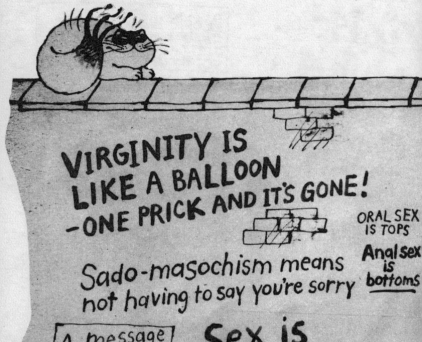

VIRGINITY IS
LIKE A BALLOON
—ONE PRICK AND IT'S GONE!

ORAL SEX
IS TOPS

Anal sex
is
bottoms

Sado-masochism means
not having to say you're sorry

A message
to all virgins
—Thanks for
nothing!

Sex is
good for two

CUNNILINGUS IS A REAL
TONGUE-TWISTER

91

I SEE MY GIRL REGULARLY—
BUT THERE'S NO HARD FEELINGS

Bestiality is going to the dogs!

ONLY RIGHT ONES DRINK MARTINI!

Yorkies are made in York— good job they weren't made in Goole!

> VAT 69 ISN'T A DRINK
> —IT'S A TOPSY-TURVY TAX

SEX IS ALL-EMBRACING

Please think again, Veronica.
I find it hard to accept 'sod off' for
an answer to my proposal. .

I'm so unlucky.
I even get caught
writing graf

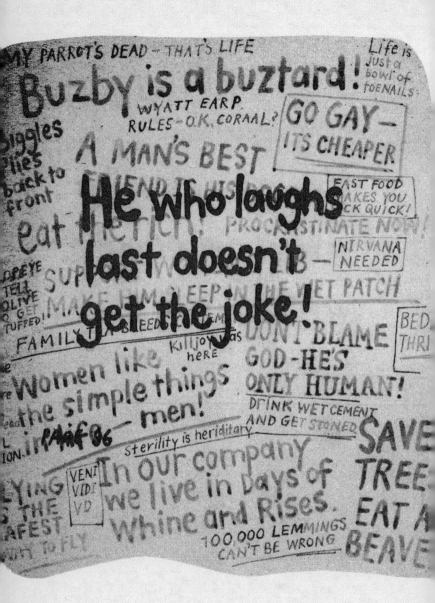